THE PROVERBS PROJECT

Head To Toe Devotions for the Whole Family

A fun-filled way to connect with God
and your family!

Allison Richmond Schoonmaker MAMFC, LPC
and Christine Coleman Varnado, MAMFC, Th.M. LPC-S

First paperback edition May 2023

Illustrations copyright © 2023 by Kristin McNess Moran

Cover design by Sara Chialastri

ISBN: 978-1-955051-15-6

Published by Punchline Publishers

**PUNCHLINE
PUBLISHERS**

www.punchlineagency.com

www.springlifecounseling.com

www.healingheartscounselingla.com

DEDICATION

*T*o *our parents:* Your love and faith have given us such firm foundations for our lives.

To our husbands: Thank you for your unending support and encouragement as our little project stretched from months into years. Thanks for keeping us going in all the ways that only y'all can do.

To our boys: Every bit of life is more fun and exciting because of y'all, the Unsafe Nature Boys.

CONTENTS

POEM

Christ Has No Body,

Teresa of Avila (1515–1582)

Christ has no body but yours,

No hands, no feet on earth but yours,

Yours are the eyes with which he looks

Compassion on this world,

Yours are the feet with which he walks to do good,

Yours are the hands, with which he blesses all the world.

Yours are the hands, yours are the feet,

Yours are the eyes, you are his body.

Christ has no body now but yours,

No hands, no feet on earth but yours,

Yours are the eyes with which he looks

Compassion on this world.

Christ has no body now on earth but yours.

PREFACE

From a young age, both of us (Christine and Allison) independently started praying that God would give us wisdom. Our desire was that we would stay on the right path, honor God with our lives, and avoid pitfalls. This was all cultivated by our early appreciation of Scripture, by our parents who were invested in the things of God, and by the many other godly influences who poured into our lives. God grabbed hold of our lives early on, and we have never let Him go.

Our desire for the families who engage in this connection-centered devotional would be that they are motivated, encouraged, and equipped to seek and apply godly wisdom to their everyday lives. We also pray this devotional would help establish parents as healthy spiritual leaders in their child's life, further pointing them to the perfect, loving, all-wise Father. As licensed professional counselors, we want to help bring connecting family principles and godly wisdom together in a fun way. Afterall, when you pair learning with healthy connection, awesome growth transpires!

HOW TO USE THIS BOOK

Step 1: Identify who you are going to team up with. This will be your Wisdom Partner or partners. Some examples of a Wisdom Partner might be a parent, older sibling, or caring adult in your life who can complete this book with a child. While this book focuses primarily on growing in wisdom, it's also an opportunity to intentionally connect with someone you care about.

Step 2: Decide when you want to do it. There are 30 devotionals so you can decide how often and when you want to do it. Some families might do one devotional a night for 30 days straight, while it may work best for others to do one devotion a week. It's up to you! We just suggest you make a plan and stick to it!

Step 3: Get the book, open it, and read it. It's that simple!

Each entry has a verse from Proverbs, then a short devotional on that verse. The **Pray** section is a prayer you can pray to God to help you apply that specific Proverb. The **Discuss** portion is where you'll talk with your Wisdom Partner about the Proverb. The last part is **Do**. This section provides a quick way to help you put into practice the wisdom from Proverbs. If your family is into social media, parents can post your daily activity from each "Do" section to Instagram with #proverbsproject and tag us at @the_proverbs_project so we can see it!

Have fun!

INTRODUCTION

What's the deal with wisdom anyway? According to the Illustrated Bible Dictionary, wisdom is defined as, "knowledge guided by insight and understanding with reverence of God as the source of wisdom." The Bible has a LOT to say about wisdom with a heavy emphasis on pursuing it. Here are some of our favorite passages:

God said King Solomon could ask for anything he wanted. Out of everything in the world he could ask for, Solomon asked for wisdom. This brought God so much joy that he made him the wisest person on earth and decided to bless him in many other ways, too (1 Kings 3:10-12).

The fear of the Lord is the beginning of wisdom. Proverbs 9:10

The beginning of wisdom is this: Get Wisdom. Though it cost all you have, get understanding. Proverbs 4:7

If any of you lacks wisdom, you should ask God, who gives generously to all without finding fault, and it will be given to you. James 1:5

It's clear that God desires for us to be wise. If we seek wisdom, he promises we will find it. If we ask for it, He will deliver! What great news!

In this 30-day devotional, we consider the question: **What would it look like to practically pursue wisdom from head to toe?** So, you'll find six devotionals each through different body parts discussed in the book of Proverbs: EYES (how you view the world), MOUTH (the words you choose), HANDS (what you give your efforts to), HEART (the core of who you are), and FEET (where you intend to go).

Each day, families will have a chance to process the practical pursuit of wisdom through a reading centered on a Bible verse and body part, a guided prayer prompt, connection-focused discussion questions, and a short activity that brings it all together.

Letter to Parents

Dear Wisdom Partners,

What a joy and privilege to partner with as you walk with your child through the book of Proverbs! Both of us (Allison and Christine) have seminary degrees and are licensed professional counselors in Louisiana. We brought our knowledge and passion of pursuing God and our understanding of psychology together in this book. As we wrote this devotional, our prayer was that we would not take lightly the task of helping families seek and find godly wisdom. We also prayed that through this journey each child would develop deep connections with their Wisdom Partner—the parent or mentor doing this book with them. We hope that together, you and your child would understand more fully what it is to seek God and be wise in Him. Before you get started, there are few concepts we'd like to unpack so you can best take on the role of your child's Wisdom Partner. They include 1) making connection a priority, 2) seeking to motivate your child in an effective way, 3) setting up your time together for success and retention, and 4) having a healthy mindset of approaching godly wisdom. 1) Connection is one of our deepest needs as humans. When we pursue connection with our children, we increase their sense of security, are able to be more influential in their lives, and help them understand a loving God. Throughout the devotional, we'll provide connecting activities to complete with your child in the "pray, discuss, do" section of each day.

Other ways to facilitate connection with your child are eye contact, healthy physical touch, and kind communication. These are simple, but powerful ways you can connect with your child. Whether it's rubbing your child's back as you read, matching your body with the way that your child is sitting, or looking at them with soft eyes as you ask questions, these can all facilitate a deep sense of connection with your child. We are more likely to joyfully listen and obey people we know care for us. Connecting is a powerful skill we hope strengthens as you do this devotional together.

As a side note, if you've experienced a negative upbringing with little connection, you may find that these skills are challenging for you. To that we first say, we are sorry that you did not have a great model for parenting and for how that has negatively impacted your life. Secondly, there is help and hope for recovering from a challenging past. We serve a God who makes all things new and loves you to the full capacity! There are also trained Christian counselors who can help you work through your past to help it stop impacting your present and future to such a degree.

2) Another influencing factor in helping the principles of this book and godly wisdom really stick with your child is to consider how a child is motivated. In the mental health field, we

refer to it as intrinsic and extrinsic motivation. Extrinsic motivation comes from an external motivator, whether that is a prize to be achieved or a negative consequence to avoid. Intrinsic motivation comes from within. It's a deep sense of being motivated to do things because of personal values, internal positive thoughts, feelings, or assigned meaning.

For example, we can motivate a child to do homework by offering a reward for finishing (like ice cream) or offering a negative consequence for not finishing (like not being able to have friends over). That's called extrinsic motivation. Intrinsic motivation would look like encouraging your child to do her homework by asking her to recall what it felt like last time she successfully completed her homework. It could also look like helping her notice some of the natural consequences of successful completion such as understanding the concept better, feeling better prepared at school, and not having to feel nervous about whether or not the teacher would check homework. Noticing these natural, positive consequences would help develop intrinsic motivation in your child.

When we encourage our children to be more intrinsically motivated, we build the higher functioning, more mature portion of their brain which has many rewarding benefits. These include things like impulse control, problem solving skills and emotional stability. It also equips our children to make good choices in and out of our presence.

Intrinsic motivation considers natural consequences, pays attention to the present moment, and creates meaning and context for our actions. It's probably obvious, but we want our children to be intrinsically motivated. This sets them up for integrity. Kids can make wise choices not because they know their parents would get them in big trouble if they made a poor choice, but because they serve a God who loves them and who is worthy of obedience. In helping your child understand the why behind obedience and seeking wisdom from God, they become more willing to apply these principles.

3) Being calm is a key indicator in being able to learn and retain information well. If your heart is racing or if you are nervous about something, your brain has too many resources in use to actually store what you're learning. Keep this in mind as you are deciding when to read this devotional. If it's on the cusp of a particularly stressful homework time, sibling argument, or anything else emotionally charged, know that sometimes you might need to help your child settle down or allow them to talk about something that's bothering them before embarking on this time together. Make connecting a priority and keep your expectations in check as you plan to read this devotional.

4) As a final exhortation, we hope you keep the promise from James 1:5-7 in mind:

If any of you lacks wisdom, you should ask God, who gives generously to all without finding fault, and it will be given to you. But when you ask, you must believe and not doubt, because the one who doubts is like a wave of the sea, blown and tossed by the wind. That per son should not expect to receive anything from the Lord.

If we ask believing, God gives wisdom generously! Let's be faithful to cling to that promise in a world that seeks wisdom from so many ungodly sources. Let's pursue God fervently with the glorious hope that He will do what He says! The efforts are ours, the outcomes are God's.

Keep in mind that actions really do speak louder than words. Let your kids see you seeking God's wisdom and His ways. In this regard, you may need to recognize your own need for repentance. Have you been valuing God's wisdom, opinions and insights above all others? It's hard to hear God when we aren't pursuing our connection with Him. To love Him is to not forget about Him! If you've been negligent in this way, repent, turn and rest in God's forgiveness.

You are taking on a noble task in helping your kids see that there is another way to live. They get enough messages daily of, "put your own desires first," "take the easy way out," and "do what makes you happy." Offering up the alternative, godly worldview is indeed countercultural, but we know that your efforts in this endeavor will never be wasted.

What a privilege that we would be able to guide our children to know our God better and live the life He has designed for them. We hope you enjoy being your child's Wisdom Partner, and it is not just a role you take for the purpose of this book, but a lifelong commitment to helping your child grow in faith.

In Christ,

Allison and Christine

Letter to Kids

Dear Kids,

We are so excited to walk with you along this journey of seeking wisdom from God! There's a story in the Bible about a man named Solomon who had recently become king of Israel (you can find it in 1 Kings 3:1-15). God visited him in a dream and told Solomon that he could ask for anything he wanted. Do you know what Solomon asked for? Not tons of money. Not a super cool chariot to be pulled by horses (I guess that would be comparable to a fancy car). Not that all his enemies would die. Not for superpowers. Solomon asked God for wisdom! What a request!

Solomon wrote most of the book of Proverbs in the Bible, which is referred to as the book of wisdom. His entire kingdom was blessed because of the wisdom of God that Solomon had.

God tells us in James 1:5 that if we lack wisdom, we can ask God who will give it to us abundantly. While superpowers, wealth, a cool car, and no enemies do sound rather attractive; wisdom is of greater value.

The ability to know right from wrong and make good choices, even when it seems confusing, will literally benefit us for a lifetime. More importantly, as we seek wisdom, we bring glory to God which is our ultimate purpose as Christians. Godly wisdom cannot be attained without first having a personal relationship with God as your Lord and Savior.

It's also really hard to be wise when we are doing things that go against God. Are there actions, thoughts, or attitudes in your life that you need to change so that from your head to your toe from your heart to soul, you honor God?

This book is designed to be done with a Wisdom Partner, so find a parent or mentor to go through this book with you. That's your Wisdom Partner! You can read it together and participate in the suggested activities together each day.

Each entry has a verse from Proverbs, then a short devotional on that verse. The **Pray** section is a prayer you can pray to God to help you apply that specific Proverb. The **Discuss** portion is where you'll talk with your Wisdom Partner about the Proverb. The last part is **Do**. This section provides a quick way to help you put into practice the wisdom from Proverbs.

We pray you trust in God's desire to give you wisdom, and that you actively pursue it not just as you go through this book, but for the rest of your life.

Sincerely,

Allison and Christine

EYES

In this section we will look at what the book of Proverbs has to say about our eyes. "Our eyes?!" you ask?? Yes! These verses will teach us about how we see the world and those around us. So grab your Wisdom Partner and open up those peepers! Remember, if your family is into social media, don't forget to post your daily activity from each "Do" section to Instagram with #proverbsproject and tag us at @the_proverbs_project so we can see it!

1) Ask the Expert

*Do not be wise in your own **eyes**; fear the Lord and shun evil.*

Proverbs 3:7

It is really easy to think that we've got things figured out and that we know best. That's what Solomon meant when he spoke about being wise in your own eyes. However, he makes it clear that we are not supposed to pretend like we know it all, but instead we should fear God.

Often when we fear something, we want to run away, but the Bible suggests the opposite. Fearing God looks like having a deep respect for His mighty power, running **to** God, and trusting and obeying His ways as best for our lives. Fearing God is an awareness of His greatness and our need for Him.

If a doctor asked me to help him perform surgery, I would cling to that surgeon's every word and every direction because I'm no surgery expert! I recognize the surgeon as the expert and know that there is no way I can effectively do a surgery without very clear guidance from him.

Similarly, we can approach God in that way. He is the LIFE expert! We NEED His guidance. Recognize that God is wiser than you and that you need Him.

Pray: God, help me not to be wise in my own eyes. Thank You for being so good and for being the life expert. Help me to seek Your wisdom and avoid evil things that don't honor you. Amen.

Discuss: Solomon goes on in Proverbs 3:7 to add a second command for fearing God. What does he suggest? Tell your Wisdom Partner what the verse says in addition to fearing God. He talks about running away from evil. Look at your Wisdom Partner and say, "evil is bad for me!" Spend some time discussing what fearing God looks like to you.

Do: List practical ways you can run away from things that aren't good for you.

NOTES

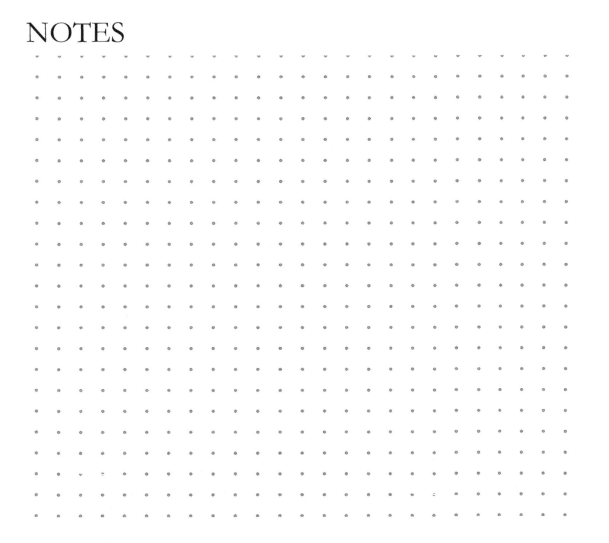

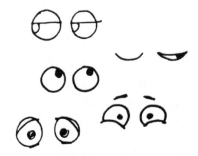

2) Eye See What You Did There

*The **eyes** of the Lord are everywhere, keeping watch on the wicked and the good.*

Proverbs 15:3

Have you ever felt like you were getting tired of making good choices, and it seems as if those who aren't making good choices are getting more attention or praise? You might be thinking, "do my good choices even matter?".

In today's verse we find our answer: Absolutely, your good choices definitely matter! God sees your good choices. Know that God is always honored when we obey Him. Your pursuit toward right living, though sometimes not recognized by other people, is always recognized by God. There is assurance in knowing that there is a God in heaven who sees all things and knows all things!

Perhaps something unkind or evil has been done to you in secret. You may think, does God even care about that? God definitely cares! Nothing goes unnoticed by our God. We can trust that God will judge between right and wrong. He rewards the good and brings justice to wrongs done to us.

In Isaiah 55:8-9, God reminds us that His thoughts and ways are not our thoughts and ways, and that His thoughts and ways are higher than ours. Even though it may not make sense or may not be super obvious that God's eyes are on the good and bad, we can trust that it's true. Oftentimes, God accomplishes things differently than we'd ever expect and in a much different time frame than we'd assume.

As counselors who get to work with people who have experienced trauma, we find this verse incredibly hopeful. Trauma is something hard that has happened to someone that causes lots of hurt in your body, mind or heart. If you've experienced trauma, we hope you know you are seen and loved by God. What hurts us, hurts God. Be brave and talk to an adult about what happened. God will make all things right when Jesus comes again!

Pray: God, thank you for seeing and knowing all things. Thank you for making a plan to make all things right. Help me to trust that your eyes see all the evil and the good. Keep this in the front of my mind as I go about my day. Amen.

Discuss: Tell your Wisdom Partner about something unkind someone did to you that no one knew about. Then tell of something kind you did that went completely unnoticed. What's it like to know that God sees all things?

Do: Try to notice something kind that someone in your family does and show appreciation.

NOTES

-WOW!

3) Prepare to be Amazed!

*My son, give me your heart and let your **eyes** delight in my ways.*

Proverbs 23:26

Great news alert from today's verse! When you grow in your love for God, you will begin to notice really amazing things. Here, God is saying: Notice my ways. Be amazed!

Picture this: the God of the whole Universe bends down, pulls your face close to his, and whispers something very, very incredible, just to you. What is it? What is so important that He wants to bring you near to tell you? He has this to say: "if you give me your heart, what you see me do in your life will AMAZE you." Pretty cool, huh?

Jeremiah says it this way: Call to me and I will answer you and tell you great and unsearchable things you do not know (Jeremiah 33:3). The closer you get to God, the more awesome things God will show you.

When you seek God, He promises you will find Him (Jeremiah 29:13). God's ways are perfect. The more you love God, the more you believe God, and the more He will show you His perfect ways.

It's hard to trust someone that we don't know. It's like that way with God, too. If we want to learn to trust Him more, we need to learn more about His character. So how do we even do that? The Bible is the best source to learn about God! Praying is another great way to learn about God. When we pray, we're talking and listening to God.

Pray: Thank God for creating you in just the right way that He knows exactly how to communicate with you. Ask Him to speak to your heart this week in special ways. Amen.

Discuss: What is something that you want to know God's opinion on in your life?

Do: Close your eyes. Put your hand as close to your cheek as you possibly can without touching. God is THAT CLOSE to you. How does that make you feel? What does He have to say?

NOTES

4) Eye Want What's Best for You

*Death and Destruction are never satisfied, and neither are human **eyes**.*

Proverbs 27:20

Do you ever feel like you just can't get enough of something? Maybe you feel that way about your favorite meal or candy. You can never have enough! Or maybe it's your favorite video game or television show. "Just one more episode, Mom!" Our verse teaches us that human eyes are never satisfied.

Sometimes we have a hard time limiting ourselves, especially when we really love something. Even if we know something isn't the healthiest or best for us, we can still have a hard time telling ourselves, "no!"

"Carnival belly" is a funny term used to describe that sick feeling in your stomach when you've gone overboard eating a bunch of delicious treats. It tastes so good going down, but all that sweet stuff can give you a major belly ache!

Whether it's candy or your favorite video game, your brain may tell you that it's a good idea to keep taking in more and more. Wisdom tells us that "more" may not always be the best choice. God can help you set boundaries or limit yourself so that you can enjoy the good gifts in your life instead of overindulging.

Pray: Pray for God to help you be wise and use your brakes even when you don't want to stop. Ask God to help you know where you need to set limits in your life. Amen.

Discuss: What areas of your life do you have a hard time telling yourself, "No!" or "Stop." or "That's enough!"? Talk with your family about coming up with a plan to choose what's best, even when your brain is saying to "keep going."

Do: Draw a picture of a stop sign, to remind yourself that you can choose to stop before you make a choice that isn't good. Hang the picture in the room where you need the most reminders to practice limits.

NOTES

5) Eye Spy: You!

Those who give to the poor will lack nothing, but those who close their **eyes** to them receive many curses.

Proverbs 28:27

In God's kingdom, sometimes things are upside down. Do you want to be great? Then be humble (James 4:10). Do you want to be a leader? Try being a servant (Mark 9:35). Do you want to gain eternal life? Be willing to give your life to God (Matthew 16:25). In today's Proverb, we see another upside-down thing: Do you want to have all that you need in life? Then find ways to give to others.

The Apostle Paul says in Philippians "And my God will meet all your needs according to the riches of his glory in Christ Jesus." (Philippians 4:19). When God is your King, He takes care of your needs. How awesome! Thank you, God!

One thing that is very cool about being in God's kingdom is that sometimes He uses the people in His kingdom to provide for each other's needs. If you use your eyes to keep on the lookout for people who may need some extra help, you will find that you have all you need as well.

When we notice needs and ignore them, that's not a reflection of how things work in God's kingdom. God is always on the lookout for how to meet our needs. And we can be like God when we keep on the lookout to meet needs, too!

Pray: God, show us how we can join you in taking care of other people's needs. Amen.

Discuss: Talk about taking care of other people's needs with your family. Who do you know who may need a little help or encouragement?

Do: Come up with a plan of how you can make your idea a reality!

NOTES

6) God Goggles

The poor and the oppressor have this in common: The Lord gives sight to the eyes of both.

Proverbs 29:13

Huh??? That's what you might be thinking after reading this verse. What does that verse mean and how in the world do you expect me to apply that to my life? Well, think of it this way, when the verse mentions the poor and the oppressor, you can think of the difference between the rich and the poor, or those in need versus those with great power. By our own worldly standards, that difference is pretty big! It's like the difference between people who have their own personal airplane to fly them around and multiple large houses versus someone who can fit all their clothes in a grocery bag without enough money to buy a car. Those people are very different, you might say!

The wonderful hope in this verse is the reminder that whoever you are, however much money you may have, whatever kind of power you have, God is the One who gives us life or, like the verse says, gives sight to our eyes! God fairly judges all people. He is the same God to the rich and the poor, the kid with good grades and the one who is failing, the kid striking out and the one hitting home runs. Similarly, God equally loves everyone. He loves the kid with the brandless backpack as much as He loves the kid with the coolest backpack.

So, here's the big deal about that verse: if God is the same God to everyone no matter what, then why are we so quick to judge or place value on people based on their grades, financial status, or who they know? When we look at people with the eyes God has given us, be reminded that God loves them all, and so should we! This kind of perspective should greatly change how we treat people and how we talk about people. And guess what? You are no exception to God's love! There is nothing you can do to make God love you more and there is nothing you can do to make God love you less. May we see people as God does, remembering God's love is the great equalizer.

Pray: God, remind me that you give sight to everyone, and help me to love people like You do. Amen.

Discuss: Ask your family to think of a time they judged someone based on worldly standards instead of godly standards.

Do: Think of someone that is most different than you, then think of 5 things you have in common.

NOTES

MOUTH

In this section we will look at what the book of Proverbs has to say about our mouths. Spoiler alert: it's more than just about brushing your teeth! The verses in Proverbs about mouths and tongues will teach us about using wisdom with the words we say. As therapists, we believe that it's important to say what you need to say, but to do so in a way that is loving and wise. So grab your Wisdom Partner and get to talkin'!

Remember, if your family is into social media, don't forget to post your daily activity from each "Do" section to Instagram with #proverbsproject and tag us at @the_proverbs_project so we can see it!

7) Sticks and Stones Say What?!

The soothing tongue is a tree of life, but a perverse tongue crushes the spirit.

Proverbs 15:4

Another translation of the Bible (The Message) puts it this way: Kind words heal and help; cutting words wound and maim.

This verse makes it clear that we have two choices with the words we speak: help or hurt.

Have you ever heard the old saying, "sticks and stones may break my bones but words will never hurt me?" As it turns out, that's not actually true! The Bible says that words can cut, wound, crush, or hurt. They may not do so physically, but they really can wound the heart. Did you know that wounds like that can last even longer than a bruise or cut? I bet your parents could think of something unkind that someone said to them when they were younger, even though it was said quite a few years ago!

As people in God's family, it's extra important to make every effort to use words that do good to the hearer. Build up, encourage, protect, show compassion, bless. These are all ways we can use our words to speak LIFE into our friends, families, and those we meet along the way. Being a person who uses words for good and not harm is one way people will know you are in God's special family.

Pray: God, help me notice opportunities to speak positive words instead of negative words to the people in my life. Amen.

Discuss: What are some times you felt the wounds of negative words that someone has spoken?

Do: What are some ways you can speak life into someone today? Make a list of 10 phrases you could be ready to use at any time.

For example: I like when you take initiative!

NOTES

8) To Say the Least

Even fools are thought wise if they keep silent, and discerning if they hold their tongues.

Proverbs 17:28

Have you ever been around someone who keeps talking and talking and talking and talking? Long after anyone is still interested? The book of Proverbs is full of comparisons between what wise people do and what foolish people do. This verse is another opportunity to compare and contrast the two. Here the Bible tells us that there is wisdom in knowing when to keep your mouth shut. "God gave you two ears and one mouth for a reason!" That kind of sounds like something a Grandpa might say! Haha.

Most people like to share what they know about a topic. It feels good to sound important and knowledgeable! But it takes humility and self-control to listen to what others have to say. So, if wise people exercise humility and self-control in situations, fools jump in and talk up a storm. In another wisdom book in the Bible that King Solomon wrote, he states it this way, "the more the words, the less the meaning, and how does that profit anyone?" (Ecclesiastes 6:11).

If you want your words to benefit those who listen, choose them wisely and know when to use them. Sometimes silence and listening is your best bet!

Pray: God, help me be wise and not foolish when I speak and when I listen. Amen.

Discuss: Ask your family members about a time when they said too much and regretted it. If you could go back and change it, what would you do differently?

Do: What might be a signal that your family could give one another if they think it's the wiser choice for you to listen?

NOTES

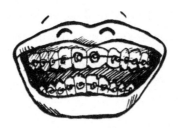

9) There's Something to be Said Here

Those who guard their mouths and their tongues keep themselves from calamity.

Proverbs 21:23

Wow, who knew the Bible spoke of the importance of mouthguards. I didn't realize Solomon valued teeth so much. Just kidding! That's not what this verse is referencing. While wearing a mouthguard to protect your teeth and jaw in sports is a good idea, watching all the words that come out of your mouth is an even better idea. Our words are powerful tools that can be used to destroy or build!

Calamity is a big word for trouble or disaster. At first glance, this verse seems like a simple task with a big promise. Watch your words and you will stay away from disaster. Okay, that makes sense. Keep this in mind though; the average human speaks at least 7,000 words per day, and some studies even suggested the average is closer to 20,000 words per day. That's a lot of words to keep in check!

Jesus gives the best motivation for keeping our words in check in Matthew 12:36, "But I tell you that everyone will have to give account on the day of judgment for every empty word they have spoken." If we would filter our words through only what God deems good and acceptable, our speech would sound much different. Gossip, lies, negative talk, harsh put downs, and unproductive words with no value would have no place in our conversations.

Pray: God, I ask you to help me filter my words with only what is honoring to you. Help me to be mindful of the things I say, and help me to know when I shouldn't say something. Amen.

Discuss: Has there ever been a time that your words got you in trouble? What do you wish you would have done differently?

Do: Get a piece of paper. On one side draw a mouthguard and, on the other side, draw a picture of a time your mouth got you in trouble. (Google "sports mouthguard" if you need help understanding this more.) Put a circle around the mouthguard and an X over the image of your words getting you in trouble. Hang this picture in your room for at least a week.

NOTES

10) When All is Said and Done

Whoever rebukes a person will in the end gain favor rather than one who has a flattering tongue.

Proverbs 28:23

Imagine this: a friend walks up to you at school and says, "I didn't have time to do my homework, so Sarah said I could copy hers. That's okay, right?" Wouldn't it be easy to tell her, "Yep, that's okay," and agree with your friend?

Today's verse teaches us that it benefits us and others when we correct someone honestly rather than to just say what pleases the other person. Perhaps in this scenario an honest response would sound like, "If you want to know the truth, that sounds like cheating to me."

Throughout the Bible, God teaches us not to take something that is not ours and to be responsible for our own work (2 Thessalonians 3:10-13). It would actually be dishonoring to God to simply agree with your friend here even though it would make your friend happy. Not only would it dishonor God, but you'd also be supporting your friend's sin.

As Christians we are called to be bold and encourage others in doing right as Jesus did. Paul says it well in Ephesians 4:15, when he encouraged us to speak the truth in love. Our love for God and people is why we encourage others to do right, so that we can build up God's Kingdom on Earth.

Pray: Holy, perfect God, help me to speak the truth in love. Help me to be brave when I need to encourage others to do what is right, and help my love for you and people be why I do it. Amen.

Discuss: Has there been a time where you took the easy route and flattered someone rather than being honest with them? What feels hard about rebuking someone or encouraging them to make the right choice?

Do: Practice with your family on how you can encourage someone to do the right thing in love. Think of a real life example you can use to practice your loving, godly response.

NOTES

11) You Don't Say?

The heart of the righteous weighs its answers, but the mouth of the wicked gushes evil.

Proverbs 15:28

This Proverb teaches us that God's righteous people stop and think first. Righteous means behavior that is right by God's standards. Today's verse says that part of being righteous is weighing or thinking about our words or choices.

Sometimes that may look like thinking through how you're going to respond to a situation. Other times that may look like seeking God in prayer and looking to the Bible until He guides you on how to answer or what choice to make. Remember that God's thoughts and ways are so different from our own (Isaiah 55:8-9). If we respond based on our own earthly wisdom, we may miss God's best for the situation.

If we seek Him, we will find Him. God will answer! You won't even believe this, but in Psalm 34, when David declares, "I sought the Lord and he answered me," he's actually referencing a time in which he acted insane to escape capture! That is crazy! Literally! Do you think that would have been David's go-to response without the guidance of our all-wise God? He did escape capture!

God is incredibly creative and wise. He will come up with a game-plan that is so much better than what we can come up with! We are right to seek God for His response in our answers and choices, and we can trust that God will answer and guide us if we seek Him.

Pray: Perfect God, help me to trust in your guidance. Help me to seek you for answers. Show me when I make choices that don't honor you, and help me make it right. Amen.

Discuss: Are there any Bible stories of God's faithfulness (remember, faithfulness means that God always does what He says He will) that you really like (Noah's Ark, David and Goliath, Gideon's army, etc.)? Remembering God's faithfulness in the past helps us to keep choosing and trusting God in the present and future even when it seems hard.

Do: Come up with a family slogan or code word to remind each other of God's faithfulness.

NOTES

12) Who Wants a Slice of Humble Pie?

Let someone else praise you, and not your own mouth; an outsider, and not your own lips.

Proverbs 27:2

This verse reminds us about a key character trait most of us could use a little more of: humility. One author puts it this way, "Humility is not thinking less of yourself, but thinking of yourself less" (C.S. Lewis).

Everyone on the planet loves being recognized for their hard work and accomplishments. And we should be! It's okay to get praise for your efforts! There's nothing wrong with being excited to show others something you received or worked hard towards. What sometimes gets us into trouble is when we start to draw too much attention toward ourselves.

Toot Toot! We're talking about bragging! Tooting your own horn!

Have you ever been around someone who bragged all the time? It's actually kind of ANNOYING!

Picture this: Someone in your class won first place at this year's science fair. You can tell that they worked very hard on it, and it did turn out cool, but they haven't even commented on your project! They just keep talking about how they won the blue "first place" ribbon. Annoying, right?!

Today's Proverb is very clear: Let someone else bring attention to your good works. Let someone else catch you doing awesome without having to tell the whole world about it on your own. How much more meaningful is it for someone to notice your efforts without being told to praise you?

Additionally, it is really awesome to be the type of person who seeks to toot other people's horns! Being an encourager is one of the best ways to support and gain favor with those around you.

Pray: God, forgive me for the times I've tooted my own horn. Give me eyes to see opportunities to use my mouth to encourage others. Amen.

Discuss: Ask your parents about a time they saw an adult bring attention to their own good works. How did it make them feel? Tell your family about a time that you wish you had been praised for something that you did. How did it make you feel?

Do: Think of someone who has done something lately that you feel is worth some extra PRAISE! Go tell them!

NOTES

HANDS

In this section we will look at what the book of Proverbs has to say about our hands. "Oh, you mean our five fingered funny fans? Our fantastic phalange flappers?" you so keenly ask? Yes. Those are the ones we are talking about! These verses will challenge us to be wise about what we give our time and efforts to.

So give your Wisdom Partner a high five and get going! Remember, if your family is into social media, don't forget to post your daily activity from each "Do" section to Instagram with #proverbsproject and tag us at @the_proverbs_project so we can see it!

13) Work Hard, Play Hard

Lazy hands make for poverty, but diligent hands bring wealth.

Proverbs 10:4

Have you ever had a really big project, and just wished you could snap your fingers and it would be done or someone else could do it for you? I can think of a few! Let's stay in this fantasyland for a bit to imagine what that would really be like. What would be the consequences of outsourcing all of your work or just not doing it at all? Sure, you'd definitely have more time to do what you wanted to do. You'd have more time to play games, watch that movie you like, take a nap, or whatever it is that you'd like to do if you didn't have to work hard. However, if you skipped all your science projects or never did your homework, or never picked up your room, you'd miss out on learning many essential skills for life. You wouldn't be good at solving problems, and life would be really hard because of your lazy choices! And, well, that would be a problem. That's what this verse is talking about, if we are lazy it sets us up to be poor. We can be poor financially or spiritually or mentally. The hope is if we can work steadily and hard, there will be many rich benefits. The thing about being lazy: it's easy for a moment, but then sets up things to be really hard in the future.

Pray: God, help me endure the hard work you've given me, and help me to recognize the benefit of working hard. Amen.

Discuss: Think of one thing you wish you could just have someone else do for you. Now think of what you might gain by working hard and doing that task.

Do: Make up a family saying that encourages hard work, and write it somewhere the whole family can see.

NOTES

14) A Reward in Hand

*From the fruit of their lips people are filled with good things, and the work of their **hands** brings them reward.*

Proverbs 12:14

I mean Proverbs really gives us some great imagery, right?! When I read that verse I think about fruit growing from my lips. Weird!! Obviously, that's not what this is talking about. The fruit of our lips are the words that we use. Our words can be as rewarding as working hard with our hands. Think back to your younger years when you learned how to build a tower with blocks. Remember how proud you felt with each new level you built without it tumbling down. Oh, the joy! Oh, the pride! It was easy to see what the work of your hands had produced. When we use good, kind, true, and respectful words, it's similar to making something great with your hands. It's a little harder to see the reward though. When you think of rewards, perhaps you associate that more with money, or treasures from a treasure chest at school, or free dress day, or ice cream. Many times, the reward from our good words and works are not really something we can hold, but something our hearts can delight in. Things like peace, joy, contentment, encouragement, and hope are all things that come naturally from good work and words.

It's worth stating here that while good works and good words definitely honor God, we don't work our way into Heaven. Rather, we accept God's gift of salvation by putting God in control of our lives and believing that Jesus is God's Son who died on the cross for our sins and rose again. Perfect Jesus earned Heaven for us! Phew! That's good news because no one besides Jesus has done enough good works to earn salvation. Jesus replaces our hearts with His, and this reality becomes more and more evident over time. The more we allow God to transform us, good works and words come out naturally.

Pray: God, work on my heart so that my hands and mouth are used for good words and works. Amen.

Discuss: What are some signs of spiritual growth that you've already seen in your life?

Do: Make your hand into the shape of a mouth (just to keep it fun and to help you remember) and say something kind about each person.

NOTES

15) Stay In Your Lane

Do not be one who shakes hands in pledge or puts up security for debts;

Proverbs 22:26

The urge to skip over this Proverb is STRONG. Shake hands? Debts? What even? Neeeeext! But as is often the case, to get the wisdom from this Proverb, a deeper look is required.

Could it be that this Proverb is saying something to us that we've all heard time and time again? MIND YA OWN BUSINESS! Don't involve yourself in other people's business. There's an idea in healthy living called boundaries. Having boundaries means you understand what's your responsibility and what's someone else's.

In the Christian world, it's always good to keep an eye out for people who could use your help. But even helping has to be balanced with wisdom! What if someone asked you to help them with their homework? What if someone wanted you to give them your homework to copy? That's helping, right? Think again! Sometimes helping too much actually hurts. And this Proverb reminds us that helping is awesome, but you have to be WISE.

If you aren't sure, ask yourself these questions:

Is it W.I.S.E.?

WORD: Does it reflect the heart of God's Word?

INTEGRITY: Does it reflect the godly character that you want to have in all settings?

SEEK: Have you sought the Lord for His guidance?

ENCOURAGING: Does it help spur those around you to do good works?

Pray: God help me grow in discernment while helping others. Amen.

Discuss: What's a time when you asked for help but you should have just done it yourself?

Do: Make up a skit about someone asking you to do something that's really their responsibility. How would you handle it?

NOTES

16) Hand It Over

Who has gone up to heaven and come down? Whose hands have gathered up the wind?
Who has wrapped up the waters in a cloak? Who has established all the ends of the earth?
What is his name, and what is the name of his son? Surely you know!

Proverbs 30:4

This sounds like a riddle like what has black and white stripes and is red all over? A sunburnt zebra, of course! However, it's no riddle and it's not hard to figure out who this verse is talking about. The author is talking about God and His greatness!

Picture a big rock that needs to be dragged up a hill. I mean, like a really big rock the size of a car. Would you want a cat to help you pull the rock up the hill, or would you prefer a bull? I hope you chose bull! The more powerful animal gives us hope that the big job can get done. Similarly, when we focus our minds on how big, mighty and powerful God is, we can rest knowing He is able, and He is big enough for the job!

When we have big worries, big requests, or are having a hard time trusting God, it's important to remember just how big, powerful, and perfectly good He is. It won't make your hard thing go away, but it makes trusting Him a little easier.

So go ahead and sing it, you know you were already thinking it, "He's got the whole world in His hands. He's got the whole wide world in his hands…" This song is a great reminder of how big God is and how small we are in comparison. God is worthy of our trust!

Pray: God, You are mighty! There is nothing too hard for You! Help me trust you more. Amen.

Discuss: When you think of God as big enough to hold the whole earth, how do you feel?

Do: Make a list of the attributes of God that you know to be true. Hang it somewhere to encourage you to trust God and seek God more.

NOTES

17) Gotta Hand It to Ya

She opens her arms to the poor and extends her hands to the needy.

Proverbs 31:20

Hands are such a visible part of your body. Think about it, you probably see your hands more than any other body part! You use them to do just about everything! From ordinary to extraordinary stuff: you can use them to blow your nose, climb a mountain, use the remote, perform a life saving surgery, feed yourself, help someone who has fallen down - - you can use them for tons of stuff!

The book of Proverbs tells lots of ways that you can use your hands out of wrong motives. You can use them to set traps for other people (Proverbs 26:27), to do violence against others (Prov. 16:27), to choose laziness over hard work (Proverbs 10:4), to take what is not yours (Proverbs 10:2), or anything that dishonors God.

In Proverbs 31 we find that a wise woman uses her arms and hands to help those in need. You may not have many resources to give, but you can find a way to serve others just by using your own two hands. Your hands are always with you and you never have to look far to find someone to help.

Next time you notice yourself doing something with your hands, pay attention to the potential your hands have for good and evaluate how well you are using them for such.

Pray: God, show me how to use my hands to honor you. Amen.

Discuss: What are some good things that you can do with your hands that honor God?

Do: Put a sticker on your hand for an entire day to help you remember to use your hands for good.

NOTES

18) The Best: Hands Down

Honor her for all that her hands have done, and let her works bring her praise at the city gate.

Proverbs 31:31

Can you think of anyone who does a LOT for you? I'm talking about a LOT. A LOTTA LOT.

Who takes care of you when you're sick and reminds you to brush your teeth? Who makes sure you're eating enough fruits and vegetables? Who taught you how to tie your shoes and makes sure you have clean underwear?

Is it one person, a few people, or a whole group? Whoever it is, aren't you glad you have someone like that in your life? Where would you ever be without them??

Honor is a word that we don't use very much in daily conversation. So, what does it mean to honor someone? To honor someone means to point out how special a person is and take the time to appreciate them. Honor sometimes looks like using our words to appreciate someone, and it also includes showing our appreciation with our actions. Doing special things for people is also honoring to them. For instance, pulling out the chair for your mom when you're having a special meal is a fancy way of showing honor. That would make her smile!

The Bible teaches us to honor those who do a lot of work for us. The people who use their hands to make sure we have all we need -- we need to make sure they feel noticed and appreciated!

Pray: God thank you for the people in my life that do so much for me. Amen.

Discuss: Talk about the main one or two people in your life who really blow you away with all the work they put into making your life run smoothly.

Do: Take the time to show honor to the one(s) who care for you. Think up a way to bless the ones who bless you the most. If the person reading this devotional with you is one who you want to honor, you'll have to go be by yourself to come up with your surprise plan!

NOTES

HEART

In this section we will look at what the book of Proverbs has to say about our hearts. We all know it as the muscle that pumps blood to our entire body. We would all be total goners without one! Have you ever met someone who did not have a heart?! I think not!

The word "heart" is also sometimes used as a metaphor (or fun and easy way to explain something) to talk about the core of who you are as a person.

Either way you mean it, it's pretty important if you ask us!

So get really close to your Wisdom Partner's heart and yell, "I know you're in there, Mr. Ticker!" What?! You think that's weird or something?? Oh alright. But don't forget to post your daily activity from each "Do" section to Instagram with #proverbsproject and tag us at @the_proverbs_project so we can see it!

19) I Like Your Necklace

Let love and faithfulness never leave you; bind them around your neck, write them on the tablet of your heart.

Proverbs 3:3

Did you know that historically, Orthadox Jews tied little boxes around their heads and necks to serve as a constant reminder of God's words? Should we bring back that trend? You first!

What this verse is saying is that love and faithfulness should always be on your heart and mind. While we may not actually write love and faithfulness on our hearts or bind them around our necks as this verse is suggesting, we can prioritize love and faithfulness so that it's a quality that people can easily see in us.

God is loving and faithful to us (Exodus 34:6), and He desires that we love and are faithful to Him in return. Simply put, to love and be faithful to God is to not forget about Him but include Him in all we do. If we love someone, we seek to love what is important to them and to be faithful in putting that into action as well. As we love and are faithful to our friends and family, we are learning to be ever-loving and faithful to the One true God!

If love and faithfulness are characteristics of God, they should be characteristics of us, too. So, how can we do that practically?

Do you do what you say you're going to do? Do you show up when you need to? Can you be counted on? Can you choose kindness when you're faced with someone in a bad mood? Do you remember to think of others when you cut into the fresh baked brownies?

Pray: Remembering love and faithfulness always seems like such a big goal. It's impossible to do without your help, God. Please help my heart and mind to truly understand and be loving and faithful to You and others.

Discuss: Talk about a specific time when you felt really loved.

Do: Instead of tying a small box around your head, think of another way you can remind yourself to remember God's words throughout the day.

NOTES

20) Heart of the Matter

*Trust in the Lord with all your **heart** and lean not on your own understanding.*

Proverbs 3:5

In this life, there are not a ton of things you can really count on. People can disappoint us and situations don't always go our way. Always remember this, though: you can count on God. This verse reminds us that you can trust God with your whole heart. And you should!

The Bible says that God's thoughts are higher than our thoughts (Isaiah 55:8-9). That just means that He's a lot smarter than us! He has perfect insight. He's a wonderful counselor. He is above all and outside of time, so He sees everything perfectly! We can trust Him.

Just because God is so much smarter than us doesn't mean that we can't trust ourselves at all, though. Quite the opposite! God has given us lots of turning signals inside of us, like our instincts, preferences, brains, taste buds and many other things that point us in good directions! We should use those things to help us make decisions. That's why He gave those direction indicators to us!

We shouldn't ONLY count on our own selves for direction. We can use our understanding of a situation, but it shouldn't be what we put ALL of our trust in. God-loyal people trust that God will show us what is best for us and the way we should go (Isaiah 48:17). We can know that God's plans for us are trustworthy and good.

The bottom line has to come back to God. We are being wise when we use the insights God has given us while looking to God for direction. This is how we acknowledge God and He directs our paths.

Pray: Help me to recognize the direction indicators that You've put inside of me, so I can use them when making decisions. Amen.

Discuss: What of your instincts, preferences, brain, taste buds, etc. are the loudest when it comes to making decisions? How do you listen to what's going on inside of you? Talk about a decision you have coming up as a family and use both your God-given direction indicators and trust in God to make a choice.

Do: Pray (yes, again) as a family about the decision you're facing, for God to give you insight as you trust in Him. We even invite you to get in a posture of humility such as kneeling or bowing down as you seek God together.

NOTES

21) You Can Get with This, or You Can Get with That

Above all else, guard your heart, for everything you do flows from it.

Proverbs 4:23

Taking responsibility for what goes on inside of you is a very important idea. As a kid, you can't always have much say-so in what your life looks like. You don't get to say what time you wake up, where you go to school, what you have for dinner, or where you live. Bummer!

When you get a little older, there are some things you get the ability to control, but SPOILER ALERT, even adults don't get to control every part of life's circumstances. No one can control the weather or traffic or how other people behave.

What everyone *can* control is the attitude of their heart. And, GREAT NEWS, that's the most important thing for you to control! Everything in life follows your attitude. No matter what life may throw at you, you can control your response to it. This doesn't mean you have to like everything, or that everything that happens is good. But think about how much power you have when something doesn't go your way, and you decide in your heart, "I can choose how to respond to this."

What does that look like? Imagine for a second that you get your room assignment for school and realize that you're stuck with the teacher you DON'T EVEN LIKE. UGH! Your year is ruined! Here are some choices. 1) You could pitch a true fit -- crying, screaming, and kicking. Just really go for it. 2) You could draw mean pictures of your teacher when she's not looking and convince other kids how terrible she is! 3) You could decide in your heart to focus on doing your best and forget the rest. What do you think will lead to the most peace in your life? Which will lead to the most frustration? Which do you want your heart to focus on? You can't always choose your circumstances, but you can choose your heart's response. Everything in life follows your heart.

Pray: God, grant me the serenity to accept the things I cannot change, the courage to change the things I can, and the wisdom to know the difference. Amen. (Taken from the Serenity Prayer.)

Discuss: When was a time that you had a hard time choosing what to focus your heart on? Is there a circumstance in your life right now that you feel like you don't have much control over except what the attitude of your heart will be?

Do: From the example above, practice helpful, true, and God-honoring things you can say to your heart to help you have peace in that situation.

NOTES

22) What's In Your Cup?

The Lord detests those whose hearts are perverse, but he delights in those whose ways are blameless.

Proverbs 11:20

There's this riddle that's been told about a person walking around with an open cup of coffee and is bumped by another person. Coffee spills out of the cup and then the question is posed, why did the coffee spill out of the cup when bumped? You'd think the answer would be something scientific and complex, but it's simpler than that. Coffee spilled out of the cup because coffee was in the cup. Had hot chocolate been in the cup, hot chocolate would have spilled out. Had tea been in the cup, tea would have spilled out. You get the picture.

Similarly, when we are "bumped" or pressed with hard times and presented with circumstances that are challenging, whatever is in our heart will spill out. If we have gratitude, joy, and peace- that will come out. If we have dissatisfaction, discontentment, and anger- that will spill out. Our ways and behavior will reflect what is in our heart.

The Lord rejoices in our blameless ways as the Scripture says because it reflects a pure heart. When God directed Samuel to choose the next king for Israel, he saw David's handsome strong brothers and just knew one of them had to be the next king. The Lord reminded Samuel that it wasn't the outside that mattered most to Him, but the inside. "The Lord does not look at the things people look at. People look at the outward appearance, but the Lord looks at the heart." (1 Samuel 16:7).

Pray: God, show me what's in my heart, and help me to change it to honor You. Amen.

Discuss: Talk about a time that you've been "bumped".

Do: Find a Bible verse about the heart, and memorize it throughout the week.

NOTES

23) 1+1= BEAR!!!

Anxiety weighs down the heart, but a kind word cheers it up.

Proverbs 12:25

Anxiety is being stressed or worried about something. When we're anxious the same part of our brain that is responsible for keeping us safe in bear encounters or shark attacks is triggered. For real! You can be anxious or worried about a test or you can be running from a bear and it all comes from the same part in your brain. That's crazy! Right?! That part of your brain that is responsible for telling you when danger is present is called your amygdala (uh-mig-duh-luh). The problem is that your amygdala can't tell the difference between a real threat (bear attack) and something that's simply stressful, uncomfortable or hard (math test). You can see why anxiety can really weigh you down. It literally makes you have a physical response like a faster heart beat, shorter breaths, and tighter muscles. Anxiety can really impact your heart and body! Thankfully there is a "but" in this verse.

Anxiety weighs down the heart, BUT a kind word cheers it up. Did you know that you need to speak kindly to yourself? If anxiety can have such a big impact on our body, the hope this verse gives is that kind words have similar potential to impact us in a big positive way. Our words are so powerful, whether they are towards somebody else or to ourselves.

James tells us that our words have the power to destroy greatly or accomplish great things (James 3:3-6). The Bible goes on to say that we are to encourage one another and build each other up (1 Thess. 5:11). So here's the takeaway: use kind words to speak to others, AND use kind words in how you speak to yourself! Watch and see what happens when you're diligent about speaking to others and to yourself kindly.

Pray: God, help me to be aware of when I am anxious in my head or my body. Help me to change the words that I'm speaking to myself or others to be more kind. Amen.

Discuss: Think about a time when you felt anxious and think back to some things you were telling yourself. Could you have spoken more kindly to yourself? If so, what would have been a better thing to tell yourself?

For example, if you were worried about your band concert coming up, and you told yourself, "you're going to mess up, and everyone will hear your mistake." Instead you could say something like, "You practiced really hard, you can do this. You've played in a band concert before and you survived!"

Do: Grab some paper and write out your negative/unkind thoughts you had when you were anxious. Flip the paper over and write your true and kind thoughts.

NOTES

24) 525,600 Minutes

Hope deferred makes the heart sick, but a longing fulfilled is a tree of life.

Proverbs 13:12

Have you ever really wanted something for a long, long time? You know how Christmas or your birthday can sometimes seem like they take for-ev-er to get here? What about prayer? Have you ever prayed for something for a long while? Maybe you've prayed for your aunt to be healed from cancer, or for your dad to get a new job, or for your Grandpa to become a Christian? It's really hard to want something for a long time and have to wait and hope for your prayers to become reality. Today's scripture even says waiting to see what you're hoping for can make your heart sick!

Waiting in hope sure can take a lot out of you, but the Bible reminds us that it's important to not give up. Romans 12:12 says, "be joyful in hope, patient in affliction, faithful in prayer."

What happens when your longing is fulfilled? It's like a tree of life. Wait..what? Think about trees. They give shade, clean the air around them, provide fruit or nuts to eat, and even supply materials for homes. They are deeply rooted beyond what you can even see. They stand up so tall and gloriously!

The connection is this: when you hope for things for a long time, it can be hard. But when you see the longing fulfilled, it turns into a great reminder of God's goodness. He was at work even when you didn't see it.

Pray: God, help me to not give up hope when it seems like what I'm praying for won't ever happen, and help my prayers line up with your desires. Amen.

Discuss: What's the thing you've prayed for the longest, even if it hasn't been resolved yet? What is it like to wait so long?

Do: Make a list of long-standing prayer requests on one side and things God has answered on the other side. Put the list on your refrigerator so you can all remember to be faithful in prayer as you wait for God to move and be reminded about what God has done so far.

NOTES

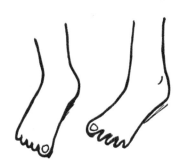

FEET

In this section we will learn what the book of Proverbs has to say about our feet. As it turns out, you're supposed to wash them. News to us! But really, these verses will help us think through where we intend to go in life.

So grab your Wisdom Partner by the foot and say, "let's kick it!"

Remember, if your family is into social media, don't forget to post your daily activity from each "Do" section to Instagram with #proverbsproject and tag us at @the_proverbs_project so we can see it!

25) #Influencer

So—join the company of good men and women, keep your feet on the tried-and-true paths. It's the men who walk straight who will settle this land, the women with integrity who will last here. The corrupt will lose their lives; the dishonest will be gone for good.

Proverbs 2:20-22 (MSG)

Did you know that needing family and friends is part of being made in God's image? One of our deepest human needs is to connect with others. That is part of God's good design of humans. The company you keep helps impact your choices. Good company =good choices. Bad company=bad choices. One secret in life is that healthy people know how to have good relationships with God, themselves, and others.

Think about this: whoever you hang out with determines what you think is "normal." In south Louisiana in late winter and early spring, we do something that is rather odd to people who don't live here. We have crawfish boils. Crawfish are mudbugs that are best described as "tiny lobsters." These delicious treats literally live in mud houses in shallow water. We catch them, boil them in spicy seasoning, then pour them on a table. Then, everybody sits around eating the crawfish. This process includes ripping their heads off, peeling the tail and slowly removing the intestine, where the crawfish's excrement is stored (that's crawfish poop that we just strip right off the crawfish tail) and pop the tail in our mouth to enjoy over and over again. A real Cajun may even suck the juices from the head. And y'all, it's delicious! Down here in Louisiana, this is totally normal. Do you have anything you do where you're from that other people might think is weird?

Do you see how much the people we surround ourselves with can influence us? The company we keep strongly shapes the way we think and how we act. They won't only influence if you think crawfish boils are awesome or not, they can also influence you in what you consider to be right and honorable choices.

Sometimes we don't always get to choose who we hang out with, like on a sports team or in your school classes, but you can choose who your close friends are. Choose wisely, knowing that they can greatly determine the paths you take. And to the people that you are around that perhaps aren't the best influence, remember that you are a representative of Jesus. That means you represent or show people who Jesus is when you act like Jesus. Stand strong against temptations that come within peers and honor God in your friendships.

Pray: God help me to seek out godly friends that will encourage me to be more like You, and help me to be a good friend encouraging others in Your ways. Amen.

Discuss: Give specific examples of how your friends are influencing you right now. It can be good or not so good.

Do: Be a good friend and think of how you can encourage your friends to make good choices. Tell your family what you plan on doing.

NOTES

26) Be Careful Little Feet Where You Go

Give careful thought to the paths for your feet and be steadfast in all your ways.

Proverbs 4:26

This verse encourages us to consider our choices and stay true to God, no matter where we are or who is watching. Some people act differently depending on the company they share at the time. Have you ever known anyone like that? They might act one way with parents, another with school friends, and another with church friends. This verse encourages us to be steadfast, steady and consistent, in all of our ways, no matter who we are with, or where we are.

Does it sometimes feel harder to honor God in front of certain people? Fitting in and not standing out is sometimes a much easier choice than being bold and sticking to your values. But this is exactly what God has called us to do. Do you honor God when your parents aren't around to see you? Do you make wise choices when the teacher isn't looking?

There's a children's song that says, "Be careful little feet where you go/ Be careful little feet where you go/ for the Father up above/ is looking down with love/ so be careful little feet where you go." God wants us to obey Him because He loves us and wants what is best for us. When we think about obeying God because He desires our best and loves us, obeying is easier. So be careful little feet where you go because our God in heaven is looking down with *love*. Trust God's love for you and that He knows what is right and best.

Pray: Perfect God, Help me to consider the paths of my feet so I can choose wisely in all circumstances. Remind me that Your ways are best! Amen.

Discuss: Think of a time when you knew the right thing to do, but didn't do it. Let everyone give their answer.

Do: Pay attention to what feelings you have when you talk about the time you chose poorly. If you haven't already, ask God for forgiveness, and trust Him that He forgives you! Tell what you wished you would have done instead. Perhaps, next time, you'll be ready to make the brave right choice!

NOTES

27) It's a Hard Knock Life

Foolish dreamers live in a world of illusion; wise realists plant their feet on the ground.

Proverbs 14:18 (MSG)

Hard work is, well, hard! We deceive ourselves when we think we will reach a challenging goal without putting in time and effort. That's the illusion that this verse is referencing. It's like saying, I'm going to be a billionaire one day, but I don't like school, so I'm not really trying. I don't plan on getting a job, and I don't have any money saved. Well, chances are that person won't be a billionaire. Right?!

In contrast, this verse goes on to teach us that a wise person plants their feet on the ground, or on what is true and real. A wise person knows that in order to reach goals, being realistic about what needs to happen is the first step.

I know a little boy who was learning to fish. He got a fishing pole for Christmas and finally had the opportunity to try it out at a pond on a camping trip. He cast at least 100 times over the course of hours that day and never caught a fish on that fishing trip. He was so persistent, but it seemed like it was worthless because he had zero fish! He did, however, learn how to cast the right way and figured out the pace at which he should reel in his line. A few months later, he was able to go fishing at that same pond, and guess what? He cast his fishing line multiple times, and he finally caught a fish! He actually caught multiple fish! It was glorious! The look on his face and the joy he experienced was a true treasure for him, and he has surely learned a lot in the process about fishing.

There really is great value in hard work. The times you will feel most proud in your life will be directly related to the amount of time and effort you put into it. If we only do the things that are easy for us to do, then we will never have the satisfaction that only hard work can bring.

Pray: God, remind me of the good that comes from working hard, and keep me focused on reaching goals that honor You. Amen.

Discuss: What's a goal you already have that you wish you could attain by *not* working for it? Maybe you wish you were a highly skilled clarinet player overnight, or perhaps you wish you've already read 100 books, or maybe you want to know how to speak another language already? Think of how you can find joy in working hard to reach that goal, and what you can gain in the process of reaching that goal.

Do: Make a list of all your family's goals, and put it somewhere for everyone to see. When someone starts struggling with it being hard, remind them that hard work is worth it and pays off. Practice telling each other, "We can do hard things!"

NOTES

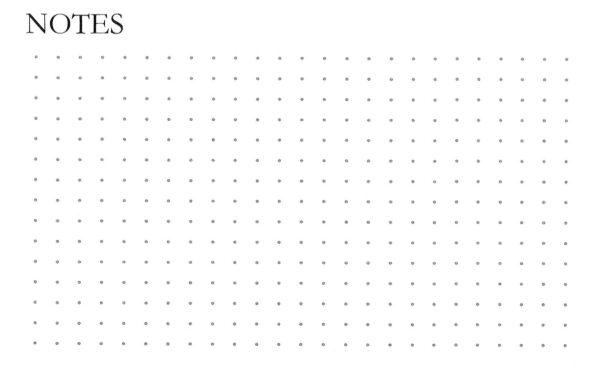

28) Do the Next Right Thing

Desire without knowledge is not good— how much more will hasty feet miss the way!

Proverbs 19:2

Do you know anyone who wants to win a gold medal at the Olympics someday? Do you know anyone who wants to be a doctor? A pilot? A teacher? What about you? What do you want to do when you grow up and finish school? Do you know what steps it will take for you to get there?

The Apostle Paul said, "Put your heart and soul into every activity you do, as though you are doing it for the Lord himself and not merely for others" (Colossians 3:23, MSG).

Have you ever thought about why you can't just start your dream job tomorrow? It's because there's a lot of learning, growing and maturing that needs to take place before being ready to start your career. There's a reason why babies can't be police officers! They couldn't handle it! Can you even imagine the chaos?!

In order to arrive at where you want to go, you have to start where you are and keep on doing the tasks God puts in front of you. Some of them will be fun and some of them will be major snooze fests. Eventually though, those tasks will all combine to lead you to the place you want to be. There are no shortcuts to important things like maturity, godliness, wisdom, or character. We just have to keep doing the next right thing to the best of our ability and trusting that God will guide our steps.

Pray: God, help me not have hasty feet that miss the goals You have for my life. Amen.

Discuss: What steps did your parents have to take in order to achieve a goal they set? What is a goal that you have? Ask your parents to help you think of the steps it would take in order to achieve that goal.

Do: Find a picture of something that represents your goal, so you can remember to keep working hard–for God and not just people–on the small tasks that will lead to achieving the big goals.

NOTES

29) I Get Knocked Down…but I Get Up Again!

Don't interfere with good people's lives; don't try to get the best of them. No matter how many times you trip them up, God-loyal people don't stay down long; Soon they're up on their feet, while the wicked end up flat on their faces.

Proverbs 24:15-16 (MSG)

What's the biggest fall you've ever had in your whole life? One time I actually fell UP the stairs. I don't even know how that's possible, but I did!

Today's verse talks about how God-loyal people may fall down, but they will get back up on their feet soon. That's talking about more than just falling up the stairs! That's talking about major life disappointments or moments when things just fall apart. But with God, the Bible says we go from "strength to strength" (Psalm 84:7). So we may be knocked down, but we will get back up by God's power that is at work within us (Ephesians 3:20).

This is one of "usually" Proverbs. It explains how things *usually* work. In this world, things don't always work exactly right. Sometimes people who dishonor God with their lives end up winning. But in the Kingdom of God, following God is always the right choice, no matter the outcome.

We will run into trouble now and again and experience things that make our hearts heavy and disappoint us. But with God on our side, we know that we can get back up again when we get knocked down and keep following Him forward. One thing is for certain, with obedience comes blessing.

Pray: God, remind me of the hope that comes from following You. Amen.

Discuss: Talk about a time when you fell down really hard. Laughing together is good for your brain and releases oxytocin, the bonding chemical!

Do: Watch a YouTube video of people falling epically.

NOTES

30) No Crazy Messengers!

Sending a message by the hands of a fool is like cutting off one's feet or drinking poison.

Proverbs 26:6

Sometimes you can read something in the Bible that instantly makes you think, "Ok that's just plain crazy!" At first glance, this verse definitely seems that way! But if you stop and think about it for a second, it starts to make sense. In a way, today's Proverb says that sending a message by a fool is just plain crazy.

Have you ever told a friend something that you didn't want anyone else to know? Maybe you took a risk and told someone something that felt special or important to you. Then, the person you told didn't value your secret and instead told other people about what you said. That can really hurt your feelings!

The truth is, not everyone is a good messenger. Next time you want to trust someone with a message, think to yourself, "is this a safe person to give my message to?" If the answer is, "no," or "I'm not sure," maybe you could consider giving the message to someone else. Don't be crazy, like the scripture says! (Haha) Your thoughts and feelings are too important to share with people who won't protect and value them!

Pray: God, help me know who the safe people are for me to share my most important thoughts with. Amen.

Talk: Discuss with your family a time when someone picked a bad messenger or a message got relayed incorrectly.

Do: Play a game of telephone within your family. How does the message come out at the end?

NOTES

CONCLUSION

The Importance of Repetition

We hope that pursuing godly wisdom is a lifelong pursuit. As most skill or character development goes, a one and done mindset just doesn't work! One great thing about families is that when one of you introduces a positive change into the system, everyone benefits! The more you prioritize godly wisdom, the more others in your family will as well. Kids can influence parents just as much as parents can influence kids!

There is so much about learning to be wise that happens on the fly. Think of how you manage conflict, stress, good news, challenges, etc. You can take just a few extra minutes to discuss concepts you've learned in The Proverbs Project as you face the regular happenings of your days and weeks as a family. As you incorporate God's wisdom into the life of your family as it naturally unfolds, godly wisdom will become part of the character of your family over time! How awesome!

We hope this 30-day devotional is just a starting point in your family pursuing wisdom together.

Wisdom: How to Keep It Going

Now that you've completed the Proverbs Project, how can you keep your family focused on wisdom?

One idea is to read Proverbs together for each day of the month. For example, on July 2, read, Proverbs 2, on October 24th, read Proverbs 24 (there are 31 Proverbs total). Imagine how much wiser you'll be in a year if you read each Proverb chapter 12 times over! Try different translations to see which you like best. We want to encourage you to continue seeking godly wisdom through God's Word, the Bible.

Another idea to keep up your wisdom pursuit is to find a Bible reading plan that fits your age and time limit or you could look for another devotional that helps you understand God's Word even more. The Bible is full of wisdom for our everyday life, but you have to take time to read it so you'll know how to live it. We pray that families and individuals would find the great value of God's Word and His wisdom, and make it a priority for life. It's worth it!

Tell us what you plan to do next on social media @the_proverbs_project. We can't wait to know how you'll continue to grow in wisdom!

APPENDIX

The Proverbs Project

30 Connecting Activities

1. Give a foot or hand massage with lotion.

2. Notice something new about your child

3. Draw an outline of a picture and let your child finish it. Encourage their effort by noticing what colors they chose and how they felt when they were done.

4. Play the hand slap game.

5. Look into your child's eyes and say, "I see your _____ color eyes."

6. Draw a letter on your child's back and let them guess which one it is.

7. Hold your palm lightly on one side of your child's face and tell her "I love you." Without giggling or laughing just a sincere "I love you."

8. "Crack an egg" on your child's head.

9. Find something new to teach your child (how to crack an egg, whistle, make gravy, make a play doh ball)

10. Ask your child what is the best present she ever received. Don't question his choice, just acknowledge what he told you.

11. Scratch your child's back with permission.

12. Play a simple game of catch with a ball.

13. Tell your child a positive story about when he was little.

14. Put a puzzle together or build a block tower together.

15. Tell your child about a time when he was really kind. Look him in the eyes when you

tell him.

16. Emphasize 3 of your child's emotions today. You felt (emotion word) when (why he felt blank). It can be positive or negative emotions.

17. Read a book, Bible verse or song lyrics together.

18. Look at family pictures together.

19. Give your child a bear hug with permission.

20. Ask for your child's opinion on something that you are willing to take her direction.

21. Take a walk together and pay attention to what you notice using all 5 senses.

22. Find something that you both think is funny. Enjoy laughing together. If you need help, try America's Funniest Home Videos.

23. Ask your child what is he afraid of? Listen without judging, just empathizing with his fear.

24. Tell your child something about them that makes you feel proud.

25. Make plans to do something together. (Actually, do it!)

26. Make a card for someone together or both write someone a card. Note how your child feels when doing it and after giving or sending the card.

27. Watch a movie. Really engage. No phones. Sit by each other or at least be in the same room.

28. Build paper airplanes together. Make this a teaching or learning opportunity (kids teach parents or vice versa). Then race the airplanes and cheer for each other's successes.

29. Each person in the family pairs up with one another; if uneven, just take turns. Have a staring contest with the following rules: you have to hold hands, smile at each other while looking at each other's eyes, and the first one to blink loses.

30. Play the "tell a story game," where each person says one sentence, then the next person adds more of the story with one sentence. See how long you can go with the whole family contributing one sentence at a time!

ABOUT THE AUTHORS

From a young age, Allison and Christine each desired lives marked by wisdom. *The Proverbs Project* is the result of this lifelong pursuit, their respective seminary degrees in marriage and family counseling, and a combined 30 years of mental health therapy experience.

Allison and Christine are both boy moms, and have been indoctrinated into the finer points of mud, Minecraft, and muscles. Allison and her husband Chad have a son and their poorly behaved beagle. Christine and her husband Matt have 3 boys and a rambunctious chocolate lab.

Allison and Christine believe family is foundational in life. If you want to change the world, start with the family unit. When parents can attune well and make healthy connections with their children, it prepares children to make healthy connections with God, self and others *for their entire life*.

What a privilege!

What a responsibility!

Allison and Christine have given their lives to equipping others in healthy connections. Healthy relationships are everything! The quality of our relationship between God, self and others is the quality of our whole lives. Their desire is that they would help others be encouraged, equipped, and established on the foundation of the Word of God.

Additional information including other written works and speaking engagements can be found at their respective websites:

Allison Schoonmaker, MA, LPC: springlifecounseling.com

Christine Varnado, MA, Th.M., LPC-S: healingheartscounselingla.com

If this devotion has been meaningful to you and your family, would you consider ordering a copy for a family that you know?

You will play a role in keeping the momentum of The Proverbs Project going. Plus, you'll help families connect more intimately with God and each other!

Healthy families. Healthy communities. Healthy world.

Scan here for purchasing options

Made in the USA
Columbia, SC
01 November 2024

44927952R00050